The Victorious

or

Spirit-Filled Life

By

J. IRVIN OVERHOLTZER

It is not the will of your Father... that one of these little ones should perish.

Matt. 18:14

CHILD EVANGELISM FELLOWSHIP PRESS

Grand Rapids, Michigan 49501

FOREWORD

It is a real pleasure and privilege to provide the Foreword to the Studies on *The Victorious or Spirit-Filled Life*. I have read the manuscript with profit. Much has been written in recent years on this important subject, but this book has the distinction of being arranged in convenient study or lesson form.

The author, like many another, passed through years of defeat and failure, wandering in desert places, before entering his Promised Land. Very aptly did Dr. C. I. Scofield say, "The experience of Christians and Christian experience are two different things."

If God, who is rich in mercy, had not brought our brother into the Land of Plenty, it is safe to say he would not have been used in so large a way in reaching children for Christ and in becoming the Founder of the Child Evangelism Fellowship. This new endeavor is much upon the heart of this man of God, and is being blessedly and widely used of the Lord.

Multitudes of Christians need these studies, which merit a wide circulation. No Christian will have much interest in soul-saving work or success in it until he knows experimentally the victorious or Spirit-filled life.

—Rev. D. L. Foster, for many years Director of Practical Work in the Moody Bible Institute.

The Victorious or Spirit-Filled Life

PREFACE

Sixteen long years of trying to keep justified by works, by service, by commandment keeping, by the observance of ordinances, with no supernatural blessing and no fellowship of the Holy Spirit, and then, by the marvelous grace of God, almost without human teachers, of coming to see the finished work of Christ, of having my soul flooded with joy and the blessing of His presence, continuing from day to day and year to year, describes one epoch of the writer's Christian life. I believe that during all those sixteen years I was a born-again believer, and for the greater part of that time I was an ordained minister.

Then another sixteen years of struggling for victory over sin, and for power in service (with more blessing in each than can be accounted for except by the unmerited grace of God), but with so much of miserable defeat without the knowledge that Christ gives victory just as He gives salvation, and that *all of grace.*

Then to come to see and to experience the freedom from the thralldom of besetting sins and receive undreamed of blessings in service sums up another period of the writer's life. Why, oh why, was I not taught these blessed truths earlier by those who were my teachers?

It is no wonder then that, when I entered the life of victory, my heart went out to the many who, like me, had failed to be taught adequately about it. Neither is it strange that the writer experienced a definite call from God to prepare a series of Bible studies on the Victorious Life, in order that others might be assisted into this life of blessing, instead of being allowed to vainly seek it, as did I, for so long a time. As I look back upon my experiences, I feel convinced that I had on two separate occasions entered the life of victory but, because of lack of instruction in the Word, I was not able to maintain it and did not know why I had lost it or how I might regain it. It seems to me that multitudes of believers have known the same experience.

May God bless these studies, which are all of His grace, so that in the presentation of these truths "line upon line," many may see and understand and learn to abide in the "life of faith" to His glory and praise.

As months were spent in preparing these lessons, it became crystal clear to the writer that the Word teaches victory in three distinct spheres of living and that one might enjoy victory in one of these without having claimed it in the others. I sincerely believe our Lord intends we should experience:

1. Victory over sin.
2. Triumph over suffering and trials.
3. Power in service.

In each of these spheres victory is "all of Him" — yea, *all of grace*. Surely He is "the God of all grace."

J. I. O.

Suggestions for the Reader:

1. These are Bible *Studies*. It is profitable just to read them; it is more profitable to look up and read every proof text; it is still more profitable to pore over every text prayerfully. They will yield precious results to any one who will read them *again and again*.

2. Studying these lessons under a regular leader is of untold value. Classes can be formed, large or small, for the study of these lessons, and they may be held either in churches or in homes. Such classes are *sure*, by the grace of God, to encourage *victorious* Christian living.

LESSON ONE

The Victorious Life Rests on Mighty Promises

Jesus cried saying, "He that believeth on me, as the scripture hath said, from within him (R.V.) shall FLOW *rivers of living water*. But this spake he of the Spirit, which they that believe in him should receive." John 7:38, 39. Every believer has received this Spirit (I Cor. 3:16; Rom. 8:9), so this wonderful promise is for each one, no matter how new or how weak. All the possibilities of these "living waters" are within you. Again, Jesus said, "I am come that they might have life, and that they might have it more abundantly." John 10:10. This more abundant life is for each believer, for Jesus came that we might have it. Once more, hearken to Jesus our Lord, "He that abideth in me, and I in him, *the same bringeth forth much fruit*." John 15:5. To have much fruit in our lives is the Lord's plan for us. He stands ready to make this promise true for you and for me.

1. *A life of victory over sin.* "Sin *shall not* have dominion over you: for ye are not under the law, but under grace" (Rom. 6:14). What a mighty promise, this! II Cor. 2:14; I Cor. 10:13; Heb. 7:25.

2. *A life of power.* "Ye shall receive power, after that the Holy Ghost is come upon you." Acts 1:8. This power was especially for witnessing, and the promise here is absolute. John 14:12; II Tim. 1:7; II Cor. 10:3, 4; Eph. 3:16, 17.

3. *A "more than conqueror"* life. "*In all these things*" (suffering, infirmity, persecution, life — no matter where lived — and even death) we are more than conquerors, *through Him that loved us.* Rom. 8:37; II Cor. 4:8, 9; II Tim. 4:7.

4. *A life of abiding, inner peace.* "The peace of God, which passeth all understanding, *shall* keep your *hearts* and *minds* in (R.V.) Christ Jesus." Phil. 4:7; John 14:27.

5. *A life of love.* The very love of God masters the life, so that all that is not love disappears. Jesus prayed that we might have this love. The Holy Spirit gives it to us. I Corinthians thirteen describes it. John 17:26; Rom. 5:5; I Cor. 13:1-13.

6. *A life that does not fulfil the lusts of the flesh.* "Walk in the Spirit, and ye *shall not* fulfil the lust of the flesh." Gal. 5:16. Pride, envy, anger, even irritability, are taken away. Rom. 8:4.

Notes: 1. This life of victory is called by various names in Scripture; the Spirit-filled life (Eph. 5:18), the abiding life (John 15:5), the abundant life (John 10:10), the blameless life (I Thess. 5:23), the more-than-conqueror life (Rom. 8:37), the perfect (meaning mature) life (Phil. 3:15), the wholly sanctified life (I Thess. 5:23), the life of Christ (Gal. 2:20), and other blessed designations. The idea of its being a victorious life comes from I John 5:4.

2. The victorious life is not a life of sinless perfection, for sinlessness is not attainable in this world. I John 1:8. It is a life of moment by moment victory over all known sin, over trials and circumstances, and in service. I John 2:1. It may be lost if the conditions upon which it rests are violated.

---

1. "That means putting Him first and letting Him have the whole place, letting Him be our actual life."

2. "It is a life in which we are kept from sin in our hearts."

— Dr. Charles G. Trumbull

8

LESSON TWO

The Victorious Life Depends Upon Justification by Faith

✗ Only those "born again" have the "new life" and "are alive from the dead" (Rom. 6:13), "a new creature" in Christ (II Cor. 5:17). The victorious life cannot be lived by those who do not possess the new life in Christ. Those who have received Christ have this new life. "This is the record, that God hath given to us eternal life, and this life is in his Son. He that hath the Son hath life; and he that hath not the Son of God hath not life. These things have I written unto you that *believe* on the name of the Son of God; *that ye may know* that ye have eternal life." I John 5:11-13.

God justifies (counts righteous) all who believe in Jesus, and gives each one eternal life (Rom. 3:26; John 3:36), but they must come on the ground of grace and not on the ground of works or merit. Many people make the mistake of thinking that their good works or ceremonies or law-keeping will justify or help justify them. Tit. 3:5. This is a mistake made by the Jews, for which they were rejected. Rom. 9:30-32; 10:3.

1. It is only through Christ's dying on the cross, in our place, and for our sins that we can be justified. We must come on that ground. Christ's resurrection establishes our justification, proving that God accepted His redemptive work. Rom. 3:24, 25; 4:25.

2. Justification is offered to all and is a free gift offered only by grace. Those who seek it in any other way may profess to be believers, but they are not justified — God does not receive them. Eph. 2:8, 9; Rom. 4:4, 5; 5:17; 11-6.

3. All who believe on Christ from the heart (sincerely, receiving Him as personal sin-bearer) on the ground of grace, are *immediately* justified, are regenerated, and

9

are given the new life. Rom. 3:21, 22; John 1:12, 13;
John 6:47.

4. When justified, our sins are all forgiven. Righteousness is imputed to us and we are complete *in Christ*. Acts
13:38, 39; Rom. 4:6-8; 23, 24; Col. 2:10.

5. Not only are we justified and saved by grace, but
we are kept saved by grace. Those who go back to works
in order to keep saved are under a curse. They lose their
blessing and cannot have victory until they renounce this
false gospel. Rom. 4:16; Gal. 1:6-8; 3:1-3; 10-14;
4:15; 5:4.

NOTES: 1. We are "in Christ" the moment we believe,
and all the riches of Christ are then ours, whether we
realize it or not. God is the "God of all grace" and He
lavishes His love and blessings upon those who believe.
Eph. 1:3; I Pet. 5:10.

2. The moment we believe we are born into God's
family and become His sons and heirs. The Spirit baptizes
us into the body of Christ, and the Holy Spirit takes up
His indwelling within us to guide us and give us power.
Gal. 4:4-6; Rom. 8:17; I Cor. 12:13; John 16:13.

"Let us always be clear on the fact that grace does not
mean God's offer to share a work with us. Grace is the
work of a jealous God, who must do the work alone; and
if we foolishly insist on having a share in that which is
exclusively God's work, we not only do not help, but we
hinder and prevent."
— DR. CHARLES G. TRUMBULL

LESSON THREE

The Victorious Life Involves Two Great Mysteries

A number of "mysteries" were especially revealed to Paul, the Apostle to the Gentiles. In a peculiar sense these are for us as Gentiles. A "mystery," as the term is used in Scripture, has reference to a great truth hitherto kept secret by God, but now revealed. But even when revealed, the mystery is hard to explain clearly. One great mystery is that of the Church, the body of Christ. Christ is in heaven at God's right hand. Matt. 18:20; Col. 3:1; Eph. 1:20. Wherever two or three meet in His Name, He is in their midst, yet, at the same time He has a body made up of all believers, Jew and Gentile. This is an actual body, of which the believers are members and He is the Head. His resurrection life is coursing through each of these members. This is indeed a mystery, but a mighty fact, and makes possible the victorious life in each believer, for each has His life. Eph. 3:2-10; 5:30, 32; 1:22, 23.

1. We are members of Christ's body (Eph. 5:30) by being baptized into it by the Spirit (I Cor. 12:13), and God has set each one of us in our places as it hath pleased Him (I Cor. 12:18). Thus we become the body of Christ and members in particular (I Cor. 12:27), with Christ as the Head of the body (Col. 1:18).

2. We are truly risen with Christ (Eph. 2:6; Col. 2:12), and He thus becomes our life, and our life is "hid" with Christ in God (Col. 3:3, 4). This life causes us to "grow up in him in all things," as individuals and, as a "body," to "increase" by that which "each joint supplieth." Eph. 4:15, 16. Christ loves, nourishes and cherishes the Church and will glorify it "without blemish." Eph. 5:25, 27, 29.

3. The other mystery is that of the indwelling Christ. Christ is in each believer, for the purpose of becoming the Lord and Master of each heart, in order that His life

11

may be *lived* in us. Col. 1:27, 28. The life and mastery of the indwelling Christ, coupled with the power of the indwelling Holy Spirit, lays the foundation for victorious living. I Cor. 3:16; Eph. 3:16.

4. Jesus taught His indwelling, and Paul says, "Christ *liveth* in me" (Gal. 2:20), . . . "to me to live *is Christ*" (Phil. 1:21), "it pleased God to *reveal* His Son *in me*" (Gal. 1:15, 16), and "Christ shall be *magnified in my body*" (Phil. 1:20). John 14:20, 23; 15:4, 5; 17:23, 26.

NOTES: 1. Everything is in readiness for Christ to live His life in each believer, but He regards the freedom of our wills as sacred, and until these are yielded the old life will still predominate. John 7:17.

2. Paul counted it his sacred duty to teach these mysteries and pled with the churches to pray for him that he might have "utterance" and "boldness" in proclaiming them. In our day many believers know little or nothing about them, and this very ignorance of believers makes it impossible for them to have the victorious life. Eph. 6:18, 19; Col. 4:2-4.

———————

"Victory is not 'an experience', it is not a 'blessing' (though it is, of course, both); it is Jesus Christ Himself; He is our victory, in Himself as a person. Seeing 'Jesus only' is victory."
— DR. CHARLES G. TRUMBULL

LESSON FOUR

The Victorious Life Is Governed by
Two Great Principles

We were justified by grace through faith, and we obtain victory in exactly the same way. These two great principles are abiding. "The just (the justified) shall *live* by faith" (Rom. 1:17), and if by faith then not by works. This text is quoted from Habakkuk 2:4, which reads, "his soul which is lifted up is not upright in him (that is in himself); but the just shall live by faith." *This text is repeated three times in the New Testament* (Rom. 1:17; Gal. 3:11, and Heb. 10:38), and yet how many of us "having begun in the Spirit" have sought to be "made perfect" in the flesh (Gal. 3:3). No wonder we have had little blessing and have experienced many sad failures. When we live by faith, we trust Christ alone for the power to live right; more, we trust Him to live in us, giving victory over all known sin. We know — or ought to know — that we cannot live victorious lives ourselves. He alone can give us that power.

1. In order to obtain the victorious life we must *know* of it and *believe* concerning its possibility. This knowledge and faith must come from what God's Word says about it. Our past failures and those of other Christians incline us to doubt; but if we are to live victoriously it must be by faith. Rom. 10:17; I John 5:4; James 1:6, 7.

2. God's Word teaches victory, or sanctification, but always as the *work of God* in us, and not as our accomplishment. Jesus prayed that the Father would sanctify us through the Word — we must believe the Word, then God sanctifies. John 17:17; I Thess. 5:23, 24; Phil. 2:13. Jesus is declared to be our sanctification, that is, His life in us accomplishes it. I Cor. 1:30; Rom. 5:10.

3. The Holy Spirit gives us complete victory, as we walk in the Spirit, but in order to "walk in the Spirit" we must trust the Spirit implicitly and trust the "flesh" not at

13

all. The whole Trinity — Father, Son and Holy Spirit — are active in providing us victory. Gal. 5:16; Rom. 8:4; II Cor. 1:9, 10; 6:16.

4. Victory being all of God is then all of grace, as well as by faith. It is because we are under grace that we have victory. Rom. 6:14. To go back to law methods — trying, or trying with God's help — brings miserable defeat. Rom. 7:19, 24.

5. Our "strength is made perfect in weakness" (II Cor. 12:9), that is, when we confess our utter inability and trust Him wholly, we obtain strength — His strength. Grace has no confidence in the flesh in the field of spiritual power, and that is the field in which victory is found. Phil. 3:3; Rom. 7:18; John 15:5.

NOTES: 1. A drunkard, penniless, friendless, a wreck in body, mind and soul, goes to a mission where "Jesus only" is held before him as his only hope. He is "converted" and *immediately* gets complete victory over the degrading sin of drink. This is the victorious life.

2. Respectable and cultured Christians need victory as badly as do drunkards. Grace requires what law commanded, that we really love God and our neighbor as ourselves, that anger, malice and envy be *put away,* not that we *try* to do these things. No man can *put away* these sins himself. God gives *complete* and *instant* victory in this field, the same as He gives to the drunkard. Col. 3:8; I Pet. 2:1, 3.

-----

1. "Faith does nothing; faith lets God do it all."

2. "One qualification that you must have for the victorious life is the broken pinion, the broken nature, uttermost weakness."

DR. CHARLES G. TRUMBULL

LESSON FIVE

The Victorious Life Versus Many Substitutes

The most common method of evading victorious living, which is living in the power of Christ, is to lower the standards of conduct or holiness as taught in the Word of God. Real victory demands holy living as taught by Christ and the apostles. The Word of God must tell what is sinful and what is not. A few have gone so far as to say that since, under grace, we are complete in Christ it does not matter if we sin. This position is utterly condemned by Scripture Jude 4. The "wisdom of the world" sets up standards of culture. The Church does the same. These standards are usually far lower than what the Word requires. If these lowered standards are *approximated* in the life, one becomes satisfied with himself. This self-satisfaction is pure self-righteousness of a very low order and keeps millions of believers from being convicted of their need of a life of victory that will bring true holiness. These are all of the "natural man" and of the "carnal mind," which cannot please God. I Cor. 1:18, 19, 29-31; 2:14; James 3:14, 15; Eph. 4:17, 18; Rom. 8:7, 8. Culture (I Cor. 13:1-3), even Christian culture, is nothing, without the love of God controlling the life. I Cor. 13:4-13.

1. Living up to a philosophy, or following a certain creed, is substituted for the victorious life. Those who so live are "beguiled" and "spoiled." Col. 2:4, 8-10.

2. Observing ceremonies and keeping days is the substitute with many for true holiness. Gal. 4:9-11; Col. 2:4, 14-17.

3. Visions and spiritual "experiences" where angel ministry or revelation is believed to be experienced are substituted for growth in holiness. Col. 2:18-20.

4. Ascetic practices have always been among the most prominent substitutes for victorious living. To subject ourselves to "ordinances," or rules of men, by which the body

15

is afflicted or denied things that are not sinful has a "show of wisdom," but these things "are not of any value against the indulgences of the flesh" (R.V.)—that is, in getting victory over the desires of the flesh which are really sinful. Col. 2:20-22.

5. Trying to make ourselves holy by keeping the law or even by trying to keep the commandments of Christ and the apostles in the spirit of law keeping commends itself to multitudes. They never see that God has given us something better, which really works. These attempts at law keeping are always a failure or, at best, an indifferent success. Rom. 7:6; Gal. 3:11, 12.

NOTES: 1. Being the possessor of special spiritual gifts has often been substituted for victorious living. Those who spoke in tongues at Corinth held this position. Paul told them that, though they had the greatest gifts (and tongues is not the greatest) and had not love, which comes alone through the life of faith, they were nothing. I Cor. 13:1-3.

2. Asceticism, which Paul condemns, often takes the form of demanding fasting or giving up every form of pleasure, however innocent. Where these practices prevail, they are an evidence that true victory is lacking. The Word teaches self denial of sinful things and things that hurt others, or in the interest of larger gifts or service to the cause. I Tim. 4:1-4; I Cor. 8:8, 9.

---

1. "In victory, somehow, we do not know how, the Lord Jesus Christ and the Holy Spirit deal with our innermost heart life in the matter of sin and keep us from sin even there."

2. "If we find there is something we need to do in the matter of victory, or find that the victory is becoming hard, a matter of effort or struggle, we are on the wrong track; we are not on God's basis."

— DR. CHARLES G. TRUMBULL

LESSON SIX

The Victorious Life Obtained by Two Great Decisions

Christ Jesus is our Substitute, both in death and resurrection. He was made "sin for us" (II Cor. 5:21), and we were "crucified with him" (Rom. 6:6). We died with Christ (Col. 2:20; 3:3) and rose with Him (Col. 3:1), obtaining "newness of life" in which we are to "walk" (Rom. 6:4). This new life is the life of Christ (Col. 3:4), by which we are "saved" from sin's power (Rom. 5:10). The "body" or hold of sin is thus destroyed (Rom. 6:6), and we are "freed from sin" — that is, from its power (Rom. 6:7). "Henceforth we should not serve sin" (Rom. 6:6) nor let it "reign" in our "mortal bodies" (Rom. 6:12). It is literally and wonderfully true that we need not let sin reign longer, for this is the Word of God, and the "Scripture cannot be broken" John 10:35. But experience proves that while this is so, millions of believers, truly "alive from the dead" (Rom. 6:13), find sin still reigning in their lives.

1. To get victory we must personally believe these facts, and "reckon" ourselves personally "dead *indeed* unto sin," to its power, "but alive unto God, *through Jesus Christ* our Lord." Rom. 6:11.

2. If we believe this, and desire to experience this blessed victory, the first great decision comes. "*Yield yourselves* to God — and *your members* as *instruments of righteousness unto God.*" "Neither yield ye your members as instruments of unrighteousness unto sin." "Let not sin reign." Rom. 6:12, 13. This all calls for a genuine decision of the will, by which the mastery of the life is yielded to the indwelling Christ as Lord.

3. The next great decision is to *trust* God for victory, *claim it* right now for yourself. He has promised it, "for sin shall not have dominion over you: for ye are not under the law, but under grace." Rom. 6:14. To "walk in new-

17

ness of life" we must step out by faith *expecting* the "new life" to manifest itself. Rom. 6:4. This must be done without waiting for feeling or evidence. "Living by faith" means to take God at His Word and *act* upon it. The evidence will quickly appear.

NOTES: 1. Millions have obtained victory in this way. Many others have sought it and failed to obtain it. There must have been a failure in them to meet the conditions, for God cannot fail. The frequent reason for failure is that the yielding was not complete. Nothing can be held back. Every known sin must be surrendered for God to take away. More fail because *they do not really trust God.* If we are afraid victory will not come, we show doubt and not faith.

2. Just what will happen when I become conscious of victory? The experiences differ, but two things are sure to come. At once or gradually the soul will experience the love of God, and such besetting sins as are known and have been surrendered will be taken away or, at least, lose their power and so become easy to control. The whole life will be gradually transformed.

---

1. "The first thing in the victorious life, for the Christian, is yielding."

2. "Lord, I cannot give this thing up. But, Lord, I will let you take it from me if you will do it."

— DR. CHARLES G. TRUMBULL

LESSON SEVEN

The Victorious Life and Freedom from the Law

Romans 3:19-31 teaches that we are free from the Law for justification. Grace freed us and in freeing us gave us a perfect righteousness, that which the law required. Romans 6, 7 and 8 teach that we are free from the law for sanctification or Christian living. Again it is grace that frees us and in freeing us it produces in us a life which, if lived, fulfils not the letter of the law (Rom. 7:6) but its righteousness (Rom. 6:14; 6:4). The righteousness of the law "is fulfilled in one word, even in this: Thou shalt love thy neighbor as thyself." Gal. 5:14. The victorious life makes possible this love. There really is a second thing which the law requires, namely, "Thou shalt love the Lord thy God with all thy heart and with all thy soul, and with all thy mind." Matt. 22:37. This love, too, the victorious life produces. It is given instantly, but its outworking is gradual. We still serve; we serve the same God; but now we serve Him as our Father, in the freedom of sonship and not in the bondage of a slave to law. Rom. 6:22; Gal. 4:4-7.

1. Grace produces what the law required, up to the measure of our knowledge and response, and we are still truly the servants of God. Gal. 2:19; I Thess. 5:23. We do not have sinless perfection, but we do have "fruit unto holiness" by being "married" to Christ. Grace produces obedience, and love enjoins it — grace and love are stronger than law. I John 1:8; Rom. 7:4; II Cor. 5:14, 15.

2. We are still under rules of conduct, though they are not found in the Mosaic Law (Gal. 5:18) but in "the Law of Christ" (Gal. 6:2; I Cor. 9:21). Christ's example and commandments (I John 2:3-6) and the commandments of the apostles are now our inspired standards (I Cor. 14:37).

19

3. The New Covenant of grace is one in which God puts His "laws into their mind" and writes them "in their hearts." Heb. 8:10. He does this by giving His love (Rom. 5:5), so that Christian character is an outflow of an inworked salvation (Phil. 2:13). Yet we need rules of conduct as a guide. I Tim. 3:14, 15.

4. We are not only free from the law itself, but we are free from the principle of law-keeping. Law put us under a curse (Gal. 3:10) for the slightest violation and left us condemned. We are now free from condemnation through the blood of Christ. Rom. 8:1, R.V. If we sin, we can have instant forgiveness by confession, instead of by punishment which the law required. I John 1:9. In addition to confession we have Christ as an Advocate for our sins. I John 2:1, 2.

NOTES: 1. Under grace we have a finished redemption (Heb. 10:10; 12, 14), sonship in God's family (John 1:12, 13), we have the indwelling Holy Spirit (I Cor. 3:16), the indwelling Christ (Col. 1:27), and the advocacy of Christ. Under law there were few if any of these wonderful blessings. It is the possession of these that enables us to live victoriously.

2. Now "the God of peace" is making us (a gradual process) "perfect in *every good work to do His will,* working in you *that which is well pleasing in His sight,* through Jesus Christ." Heb. 13:20, 21; Phil. 2:13. What a blessed salvation!

"The grace of God is the dynamo of heaven, working night and day, all the time, to accomplish things for us and in us that we can never accomplish for ourselves."

-- DR. CHARLES G. TRUMBULL

LESSON EIGHT

The Victorious Life and the Self Life

"Yield yourselves" and "yield your members" is the absolute requirement for victory. Christ must be supreme in the life if He is to live in us. It is the "I" in us that must yield, and this yielding must be very thoroughgoing. After we are born again, we are new creatures (II Cor. 5:17), and a new "I" has come to dwell in us. Paul said, "I am crucified with Christ: nevertheless I live, yet not I, but Christ liveth in me: and the life which I now live in the flesh I live by the faith of the Son of God, who loved me, and gave himself for me." From this text it seems that when Christ lives in us He must be completely controlling our new "I." If He is to control, the old "I" must be entirely conquered. Gal. 2:20. Our dual personality under grace is described as the "old man" and the "new man." We are commanded to "put off" the "old man" and "put on" the "new." This should be once for all if there is to be continued victory. Eph. 4:22, 24. In actual experience this process will have to be repeated. The "new man" is Christ formed in the believer. Gal. 4:19.

1. Unless the "old man" is put completely under, there will be constant warfare within, the flesh lusting against the Spirit and the Spirit against the flesh. Gal. 5:17. The "old man" is "corrupt according to the deceitful lusts," while the "new man" is "created in righteousness and true holiness." (Eph. 4:22, 24). No wonder there is war.

2. "No man can serve two masters" (Matt. 6:24); in order, therefore, for man to have victory the flesh must be crucified (put in the place of death) and Christ must be "all and in all" (Gal. 5:24; Col. 3:11). Paul said, "I am crucified with Christ"; this must be a transaction that is not up for constant debate. The Colossians had "put

21

off" the "old man" and "put on" the "new man" as an accomplished fact. Col. 3:9, 10.

3. Self is a many-sided creature. We cannot "crucify" him, but should yield him to Christ, that He may do it. To be sure that self is "made conformable unto his (Christ's) death" (Phil. 3:10), we must look him over carefully. Selfishness appears first. How true that "all seek their own, not the things that are Jesus Christ's." Phil. 2:21; I Cor. 13:5; II Cor. 8:9.

    a. Self-will is one of the hardest to yield, but it must be yielded from the heart. Full obedience depends on a surrendered will. Even Jesus surrendered His will to the Father. James 4:13-15; Eph. 6:6; John 5:30; 6:38.

    b. Self-trust or self-reliance must be yielded. In worldly things self-reliance may have a place, but in the field of supernatural victory it has no place at all. John 15:4, 5.

    c. Self-seeking — of honor, fame, position, or wealth — must be yielded to Christ. John 5:44; I Cor. 1:29, 31; Gal. 6:14.

    d. Self-pleasing must be yielded. There are many forms of sinful pleasure to which Christians cling. Luxury and ease are often besetting sins. All must be yielded. II Tim. 3:4, 5; Heb. 11:24, 25.

NOTES: 1. The sad thing is that many, even prominent Christians, are not *willing* to let Christ rule in every department of their lives. Phil. 2:13.

2. They doubt whether God's will will prove to be "good and acceptable and *perfect*." Rom. 12:2.

---

1. "If you want to be holy in God's sight you must be wholly in God's hands."

2. "If we are Christians we are going to suffer and have a hard time of it as long as we continue unsurrendered."

— DR. CHARLES G. TRUMBULL

LESSON NINE

The Victorious Life a Life of Love

Our "hearts" and "minds" are to be "kept" "in Christ Jesus." Our hearts are mentioned first (Phil. 4:7), for the first work, after one actually yields to the Lord Jesus and trusts Him as the supreme Master of the life, is to have his heart flooded with the love of God. (Rom. 5:5.) No one is ignorant of the mighty power of love, nor of its beauty, if it is a love that is pure. What human love does to the heart and life, that divine love does, only much more wonderfully. When we realize that "God is love" (I John 4:16) and that "love is of God" (I John 4:7), we should expect His control of the life to manifest itself in just this way. This love is "in the Spirit" (Col. 1:8); it is "shed abroad in our hearts by the Holy Ghost;" it is the "fruit of the Spirit" (Gal. 5:22). All this shows that this love is *all* of God, we can *never* produce it by human effort.

1. Scripture is very clear that this love is to be "put on" by us, hence, we are responsible if we do not have it. This is making it plain that victory and the love which victory brings are obtained and maintained by *our* yielding and trusting. Col. 3:14.

2. This is the love with which God loves Jesus. John 17:26. It is so necessary that it is "above all things" (Col. 3:14), and without it our best efforts and greatest attainments are "nothing" in God's sight (I Cor. 13:1-3, R.V.).

3. The measure of this love *increases* "more and more" until it will "abound" (Phil. 1:9; I Thess. 3:12), and then we will "know" (experientially) "the love of Christ," its "breadth, and length, and depth, and height" (Eph. 3:16-19). Just here it should be made very plain that *the victorious life is a life of growth and further attainment.*

4. This love first of all causes us to love God and the

23

Lord Jesus above all else, makes us keep the Lord's commandments, and takes away all fear of God. John 21:15; 14:21; I Pet. 1:8, 9; I Cor. 16:22; I John 4:18, 19.

5. It causes us to love our neighbors as ourselves, whether friend or enemy, husband, wife, father, mother, brother, sister, son or daughter. It makes us yearn for their salvation until we are burdened for them and seek them, and not only them but the children also, for they are our neighbors too. Luke 6:27, 32; I Cor. 9:22; Rom. 9:1-3; Matt. 18:12-14.

NOTES: 1. This love causes us to love our brethren in the Lord in a peculiar way, bridging all differences of race and station, and so we labor together in harmony. John 13:34-35; I Pet. 4:8; Matt. 18:21, 22; I John 4:20, 21.

2. This love is longsuffering, kind, free from envy, pride, folly, self-seeking, boasting, irritability, brooding over wrongs, complaining, doubt, and anxiety. I Cor. 13:4-7. It never fails, that is, it surmounts all obstacles, and it will abide through all eternity, for heaven is the land of *perfect* love I Cor. 13:8, 13. No wonder Jude says, "keep yourselves in the love of God" Jude 21.

"Do we need victory here? We do if we have not the very love of God shed abroad in our hearts by the Holy Spirit."

— DR. CHARLES G. TRUMBULL.

LESSON TEN

The Victorious Life and the Renewing of the Mind

The transformation which the victorious life accomplishes is "by the renewing of the mind." Rom. 12:2. "To be carnally minded is death; but to be spiritually minded is life and peace." Rom. 8:6. The mind does not renew itself; it must be renewed, and the Spirit will renew it when we yield it to Him. The very "spirit of your mind" must be changed. Eph. 4:23. Carnal minds are "corrupt" (II Tim. 3:8), full of "enmity against God" (Rom. 8:7); they are "heady, highminded" (II Tim. 3:4), "puffed up" (Col. 2:18) and full of "vanity" (Eph. 4:17). Is it any wonder that they need renewing? How many have struggled in vain to accomplish this renewing themselves or with God's *help* and failed! That is not God's way under grace. The first thing needed is "humbleness of mind" and this our victory brings to us. In yielding to the Lord to exercise humbleness of mind, we put it on. Meekness is a stronger word, including mildness of temper. Col. 3:12. The humble mind is the mind of Christ. Phil. 2:2-8; Matt. 11:29.

1. Our "knowledge" must be "renewed" (Col. 3:10), and there must be an "increasing in the *knowledge of God*" and a being "filled with the knowledge of His *will*" (Col. 1:9, 10). We "grow in grace and knowledge" (II Pet. 3:18); these two are never separated. Zeal is good but, if it is not according to knowledge, that zeal is dangerous Rom. 10:1-3. The humble mind seeks the knowledge of God.

2. By the Word of God we are sanctified (Eph. 5:26), we grow (I Pet. 2:2), are made wise and are "thoroughly furnished unto all good works" (II Tim. 3:15-17). Only by study and through teaching of the Word of God can the victorious life be lived. II Tim. 2:15; Eph. 4:11-15.

3. We need wisdom. Spiritual wisdom never comes

from the world. It comes from the Word and through experience. It comes directly from God, when we are yielded and ready to receive it. James 1:5-7; 3:13-17. God gives us "sound" minds. II Tim. 1:7.

4. Our thought life must be purified. We are to think on pure things, things that are true, honest, just, lovely and of good report. Phil. 4:8. "Out of the heart proceed evil thoughts" (Matt. 15:19), and no one but God can control our thinking. We should trust Him to do this until "every thought" is brought "into captivity" "to the obed ience of Christ." This will be gradual. II Cor. 10:5.

5. "The peace of God, *which passeth all understanding,* shall keep your hearts and your thoughts in Christ Jesus." Phil. 4:7, R.V. A mind at rest and untroubled is God's plan for us. Never by "trying" can this be brought about, only by yielding and trusting Him. Phil. 4:6, 7.

NOTES: 1. "I will put my laws into their hearts, and in their minds will I write them" is God's promise. Heb. 10:16. When these laws are hidden in the heart, we may meditate upon them and so not sin against God. Ps. 1:2; 119:11.

2. No victorious Christian dare neglect the prayerful reading of the Word. The faith by which we walk rests in the Word, and even "pure minds" need to be stirred up "by way of remembrance." Rom. 10:17; II Pet. 3:1.

———————

1. "Irritation is sin, and the victorious life means that we can be free from that innermost irritation. Yes, *free.*"

2. "Have we all realized that worry is sin — black, murderous, God-defying, Christ-rejecting sin — worry about anything, at any time?"

— DR. CHARLES G. TRUMBULL

LESSON ELEVEN

The Victorious Life and Our Bodies, the Temple of God

The whole man must be victorious, and this man includes "spirit, soul, and body." They, each one, should "be preserved *blameless* unto the coming of our Lord Jesus Christ"; not faultless, that would be sinless — but blameless, free from known sin. That is what it means to be wholly sanctified. *We* can never keep ourselves blameless, but "faithful is he that calleth you, *who also will do it.*" I Thess. 5:23, 24. Our bodies are "members of Christ," they are "for the Lord, and the Lord for the body," for at the resurrection they shall be raised by His power. "Your body is the temple of the Holy Ghost .... and ye are not your own .... ye are bought with a price: therefore glorify God in your body, and in your spirit, which are God's." I Cor. 6:13-15, 19, 20. The lusts of the flesh must be conquered, or we cannot please God. The word "lust" (meaning strong desire) is used in both a good and a bad sense in the Bible, for the Spirit lusteth. All *sinful* desires of the flesh must be conquered. Gal. 5:13, 16, 17; Rom. 8:5, 8, 12.

1. The "deeds of the body" must be mortified (subdued), then "ye shall live" *victoriously.* If you are victorious and you fail to "mortify the (sinful) deeds of the body," "ye shall die" — you shall lose your victorious power. By yielding these deeds to Him and trusting Him alone, you can conquer every one. "Through the Spirit" they are mortified. Rom. 8:13.

2. If we are "not discerning the Lord's body," that is, discerning that we are a part of the body, we can but be "weak" and "sickly" and even "asleep." I Cor. 11:29, 30. How well this describes the condition of multitudes of believers!

3. "*Every* weight" (hindrance) is to be laid "aside," also "the sin which *doth so easily* beset us." Heb. 12:1.

27

Our bodies must be brought "into subjection" or we will "be a castaway" from His blessing and power. I Cor. 9:27. "If any man defile the temple of God, him shall God destroy; for the temple of God is holy, which temple ye are." I Cor. 3:17.

4. We are still dealing with the "putting off" of the "old man," but his "members" must be "put off" too. We must "mortify" each one and do a thorough job of it. We "put off" each member by yielding that member to Christ and trusting Him to take it away. What a terrible list of members is given in this text, Colossians 3:5-9.

5. "They that are Christ's (those who have yielded wholly to Him) have crucified (doomed to death) the flesh, with its affections and lusts." When they have done this, they can "walk in the Spirit," for the Spirit will have complete control. Then "ye *shall not* fulfill the lust of the flesh" — instead, victory will be complete in the field of sinful lusts. Gal. 5:16, 24.

NOTES: 1. After promising victory, as we walk in the Spirit, the apostle contrasts the "works" or lusts of the flesh with the fruit of the Spirit (Gal. 5:19-23); then He pleads that we "walk in the Spirit" (Gal. 5:25).

2. As we grow in knowledge, though we shall still know only in part (I Cor. 13:12), we shall know more specifically what things are sinful. "Abstain from all appearance of evil" is the high goal set for us. I Thess. 5:22.

---

1. "Surrender includes letting the wrong things go out of our life; everybody knows that — that the wrong things, the things we know are wrong, or that we are doubtful about, must be abandoned wholly."

2. "You will never have the victory Christ wants you to have unless you surrender wholly to Him; and if you want it now, do it now."

— DR. CHARLES G. TRUMBULL

28

LESSON TWELVE

The Victorious Life and the Graces Which Adorn It

"Christ liveth in me" when I live the victorious life, yet the very fact that He lived sinlessly and that I do not and never will while living in the flesh should cause me to see how I may hinder the fullness of His life from dwelling in me. The wonderful graces listed in Galatians 5:22, 23 are all the fruit of the Spirit, and yet some of the very graces mentioned there we are told to "put on." Col. 3:12-14. This can mean but one thing — that, just as we "put off" vices, so we are to "put on" virtues. If we see that we lack one of the graces or that its measure is restricted in us, we must confess that need to the Lord, yield to Him, and in exactly the same way that we obtained victory at the beginning trust Him to supply the lack. It should be self-evident that any attempt on our part to add such graces as love, joy, or peace in our own strength will prove a failure. But, as we learned in our last lesson about putting off the lusts of the flesh, "faithful is he that calleth you, who also *will do it.*" I Thess. 5:24.

1. Standing next to love (studied in Lesson Nine) in this list of graces is joy, which is produced in the life by the Spirit of God. The statement, "The joy of the Lord is your *strength,*" at first seems very strange, but to be joyful in the midst of suffering, etc., certainly evidences a power, mighty indeed. This joy may be ours at all times. Neh. 8:10; Phil. 4:4; II Cor. 6:10.

2. When we are justified by faith we have peace *with* God. Rom. 5:1. Only the victorious life can bring us the peace *of God* and cause that peace to remain. Isa. 26:3; Phil. 4:6, 7.

3. Long-suffering, which victory brings, does not find fault, or complain, or grumble. When our Lord was reviled, He reviled not again; when He suffered, He threatened not, but committed Himself to Him who judgest

righteously. I Pet. 2:21, 23; 4:12-16, 19; Phil. 1:29, 30; II Cor. 4:17, 18.

4. Gentleness must shine out if Christ is controlling us, for a bruised reed would He not break. Matt. 12:20. The wisdom from above is "gentle." James 3:17. The word "bowels," used so often in Scripture, means "tenderness, pity." Col. 3:12; II Cor. 10:1.

5. Goodness is an attribute of Jehovah. It is difficult to define but easy to recognize. It is not merely passive but expresses itself in many, many ways. Ps. 33:5; Eph. 5:8, 9.

6. Faith comes not only by hearing the Word, by receiving it as a gift of the Spirit, and by acquirement through prayer, but it is one of the graces of the fruit of the Spirit. Oh, may we hasten to put it on! The need is great. Eph. 6:23; I Thess. 5:8; I Tim. 1:14 (note how faith and love are joined together in this text); Gal. 2:20.

NOTES: 1. Meekness, humility, and mildness of temper can be had by each victorious Christian. Only the power of Christ can give it. Eph. 4:1-3.

2. Temperance means being wise and reasonable, using moderation, and exercising sane self-control. It means being Christ-controlled. I Cor. 9:25.

---

1. "The lack of peace is as real a sin as any other kind of sin. The Christian who lacks peace is a defeated Christian."

2. "Is joy a fact in your life? Not a feeling, for our feelings are variable; but joy — rooted and grounded in the Rock of Ages?"

— DR. CHARLES G. TRUMBULL

LESSON THIRTEEN

The Victorious Life and the Standards of Christian Conduct

Grace has not left us without *standards* of conduct — definite, clear-cut commandments as to what is right and wrong. We are still under "obedience unto righteousness" (Rom. 6:16) and still the "servants of God" (Rom. 6:22). The commandments of Christ have taken the place of the law. This is so emphatically true that "he that sayeth, I know him, and keepeth not *his* commandments, is a liar, and the truth is not in him." I John 2:4. The commandments of Christ have been supplemented by those of the apostles, and the apostles do not hesitate to call their injunctions commandments. They put them on a par with those commandments of Christ. I Cor. 14:37. We can never "love righteousness" and "hate inquity" (Heb. 1:9) unless we have clear-cut teaching as to what is right and what is wrong. Confusion on this question is destroying all standards. We find that the New Testament gives most complete commandments and instructions for every phase of conduct.

1. Holiness is the New Testament word for Christian conduct, signifying that this conduct is the product of the Holy Spirit. "God hath not called us unto uncleanness, but unto holiness." I Thess. 3:13; 4:7. The *examples* of Christ and the apostles, together with their commandments and teachings, give us the absolute standard of Christian conduct. I Cor. 11:1; I John 2:6; I Pet. 2:21, 22.

2. General and personal sins of every kind are pointed out and rebuked, and the warning given that "they which do such things shall not *inherit* the kingdom of God." Gal. 5:19-21; Eph. 4:25-29. By putting off these sins and "walking in the Spirit," absolute victory is promised. Col. 3:5-9; Gal. 5:16.

31

3. Commandments and instructions are given on marriage and divorce, the home, husband, wife, parents, children, etc. Heb. 13:4; Matt. 19:3-9; I Cor. 7:1-17 (for home reading); Eph. 5:22 to 6:4.

4. Both employer and employee are given commandments (Eph. 6:5-9), the rich (I Tim. 6:17-19), and the poor (I Tim. 6:6-10).

5. Duty to government and the duty of government are plainly given. Rom. 13:1-7; I Pet. 2:13-15. Honesty (Rom. 13:13); industry (I Thess. 4:11); justice and mercy (Matt. 23:23); forgiveness (Luke 17:1-4); liberality (Luke 6:38); support of the weak (I Thess. 5:14); etc. — for these there is teaching, and commands are recorded concerning them.

NOTES: 1. Profanity and irreverence are condemned (Col. 3:8; I Pet. 2:1), also idolatry (I Cor. 10:14), and false doctrines in many forms. (II Tim. 4:1-4).

2. Much instruction is given concerning the officers, the conduct of the local church, and the administering of its ordinances. All this shows how fully and clearly we are provided with a code of Christian conduct, covering, at least in principle, every walk of life.

---

1. "The sin question is the central question in the Victorious Life."

2. "And sin, you know, never cures itself."

— DR. CHARLES G. TRUMBULL

LESSON FOURTEEN

The Victorious Life and Affliction, Trials, Persecution, etc.

We are wonderfully saved from sin's penalty and from sin's power, but we are not yet saved from sin's presence or from sin's effects. While we cannot be delivered from those, we are promised glorious victory over them. Romans 8:14-39 deals fully with this question. "The creation was subjected to vanity, not of its own will, but by reason of him who subjected it." v. 20, R.V. "For we know that the whole creation groaneth and travaileth in pain together until now. And not only so, but *ourselves* (Paul and every other believer) also, who have the first-fruits of the Spirit, even we ourselves groan within ourselves, *waiting* for our adoption, to wit, the *redemption of our body*." vv. 22, 23, R.V. The curse of sin is on the world in which we live, even upon our own bodies. Sinning men are everywhere about us, and the results of our past sins have to be met. If we contracted debts while we were unsaved they must be paid, if possible. Facts first must be faced, then victory claimed.

1. The creation will be delivered and our bodies glorified (Rom. 8:21; Phil. 3:20, 21), but now we have our "treasure" in "earthen vessels" (II Cor. 4:7) — some of them crippled, deformed, or afflicted. Even Paul had his thorn, which victory did not remove but *did* conquer. "My grace is sufficient for thee" is for us as well as for Paul and, in every kind and time of affliction, we should *claim* it. II Cor. 12:7-10.

2. Sometimes God heals sickness or removes the cause of the trials. This cure comes through prayer (James 5:15) and not by claiming victory apart from prayer. Many, many times He does not remove the cause. Paul suffered the greatest trials, even lack of food. Poverty and dire affliction often come to the rarest saints. II Cor. 4:8, 9; 6:4, 5; 7:5; 11:23-27; Acts 20:23.

3. Jesus said: "In the world ye *shall* have tribulation" (John 16:33), so we should not think it "strange" (I Pet. 4:12, 13; 5:9) but rather rejoice (James 1:2; II Cor. 12:10; Phil. 1:29), for it will increase our "eternal weight of glory" (II Cor. 4:17, 18). Only by suffering with Christ can we "reign" with Him. It was in this connection that it was said "we *know* that all things work together for good," for God (our Father) permits us to suffer in order that we may reign. Rom 8:17, 28-30; I Pet. 4:19.

4. We are promised "more than conqueror" grace and victory to endure and overcome every form of human trial and suffering (Rom. 8:35-39), even the trial unto death by martyrdom, and we are assured that when we are not delivered from the trial it is not because we are separated from the "love of Christ" — His love *abides* in victory, instead of in deliverance.

NOTES: 1. When God does not heal or remove the cause of affliction, it is not because there is a "charge" against us. How could God, who justified us, or Christ, who died for us and is now interceding for us, have any reason to condemn us when we are trusting Him? Rom. 8:31-34.

2. Only prayer can help in an affliction which God will not remove. We are often too perplexed at such times to know how to pray. Then, blessed be God, the Holy Spirit prays for us — always in the will of God. Rom. 8:26, 27.

---

1. "You do not know how He does it — no one does; but you know that He is true to His Word."

2. "We must surrender our past. Some of you are feeling that your past, the failures you have had, necessarily prevent the victory you would like to have. Satan is lying to us about our past."

— Dr. Charles G. Trumbull

34

LESSON FIFTEEN

The Victorious Life and the Place of Prayer

Praise for what the Lord has done must precede petition for what we want Him to do. If He has saved you, praise Him for it. How wrong it would be to ask Him to save you if He had already done so. It is the same way with victory. We should claim, or appropriate, victory and then praise God for it — even before we experience it. If you do not believe you have victory with enough certainty to praise God for it, you evidently do not have it at all. Then how wrong it is to be asking for victory that we already have. Instead, we should be praising God all the day long. "I will bless the Lord at all times: his praise shall continually be in my mouth" (Ps. 34:1) should be the attitude of every victorious Christian. Even if it is an effort to praise, "let us offer the *sacrifice* of praise to God continually." Heb. 13:15. It is the only way to keep victory. While we should not pray for the things we have, there is much, very much, still for which to pray in behalf of ourselves and others, and the victorious Christian has the fullest promise that his prayers will be answered. Is not his prayer responsibility then very great? John 15:7.

1. Because affliction abounds; because there are sinners to save and the gospel to preach; because Satan opposes every child of God — for these reasons, pray, pray, and pray. Ask largely; it honors Him. There can never be a question of His ability. "He is able to do exceeding abundantly above all that we ask or think." Eph. 3:20.

2. Seek to know God's will, and pray in His will. His promises declare His will. Often we ask for deliverance, when we should ask only for grace to endure. I John 5:14, 15; James 4:3.

3. It should be a joy to pray, as we come "boldly," because we are "complete in Him," and it can be with

35

"confidence" that we pray because every known sin is confessed. We can expect the answer because His promise is true. Heb. 4:16; Col. 2:10; I John 3:21, 22; Mark 11:24.

4. We should pray for ourselves, for our usefulness, our needs, for everything that would otherwise cause anxiety. James 4:2; 5:13; II Cor. 12:8; Eph. 6:19, 20; Phil. 4:6, 7.

5. We should pray for our fellow-believers (Eph. 6:18), for their increase in love (Phil. 1:9-11), knowledge and wisdom (Eph. 1:16-19), for their prosperity and health (III John 2, R.V.), their healing (James 5:15), and sanctification (I Thess. 5:23).

6. We should pray for souls to be saved, workers to be provided, blessing upon those in the work, etc. Rom. 10:1; Luke 10:2; II Thess. 3:1, 2.

NOTES: 1. Be "instant" in prayer — praying always, everywhere, unceasingly, perseveringly, exceedingly, in secret, in the Spirit — striving together, watching for the answer. Rom. 12:12; I Tim. 2:8; I Thess 3:10; 5:17; Matt. 6:6; Rom. 15:30.

2. Some are praying for things they should be claiming; others are claiming things for which they should be praying. Some are eager for things which they could have if they would but ask; some are asking for things which they can never have.

"There is a fighting, a striving, a contending, which by no means effortless, has a large place in the Christian life: It is in connection with the intercessory prayer life."

— DR. CHARLES G. TRUMBULL

LESSON SIXTEEN

The Victorious Life and Separation from the World

God loves the world of sinners and gave His Son to die for them. John 3:16. We should, therefore, love them also. And yet we are commanded to "love not the world, neither the things that are in the world. If any man love the world, the love of the Father is not in him." But the apostle hastens to explain that it is the "*lust* of the flesh, and the *lust* of the eyes and the *pride* of life" to which he is referring. I John 2:15-17. It is the world of sin, the world system controlled by the "god of this world" which we are not to love and from which we are to separate ourselves. II Cor. 4:4; John 12:31. To the material blessings of life there is no allusion in any way, for of these it is said the "living God" giveth them "richly" — "to enjoy." I Tim. 6:17. The idea that innocent pleasure, laughter, the play of children, clean social life, healthful recreation and the love of flowers, etc., is worldly and sinful is unscriptural and ascetic. Jesus' friendships were beautiful (especially those with Martha, Mary and Lazarus, and with John); His social contacts broad; He was even called "gluttonous" because he ate normally. Matt. 11:16-19; John 2:2; 12:2; Luke 7:36; Mark 6:31.

1. The world honors men unduly and forgets God; it builds only for time and neglects eternity; therefore, much that is sinful is condoned or even applauded. To these things we dare not conform, for we are pilgrims. Rom. 12:2; James 4:4; Heb. 11:13, 14; Phil. 3:20, 21, R.V.

2. Often worldly pleasure is entirely sinful, dishonoring God, is sometimes lewd and suggestive. Again, it may be dangerous because of entangling alliances or because it is so near the border line of sin. Such pleasure must be put away if one is to have victory. Pleasure itself is not

sinful. Heb. 11:25; II Thess. 2:12; Ps. 16:11; I Cor. 10:31.

3. Separation is demanded where compromise over idolatry or the world's false religions is involved. II Cor. 6:14-18; Gal. 1:8; II Tim. 3:5; II John 1:11.

4. Any worldly thing, however good, immediately becomes sinful when it is placed ahead of God or turns us from our duty. Gal. 1:10; I Tim. 6:10; II Tim. 3:4; 4:10. Our treasures should be laid up in heaven, and not on earth. Matt. 6:19, 20; II Cor. 9:6, 7.

NOTES: 1. There is a grave danger of becoming so engrossed in worldly things, work, business, or pleasure, that before we are aware of it we are hindered in performing our duty to God. Mark 4:18, 19.

2. God separated Israel by isolation. That is not His way now. In the family separation may be necessary on vital questions without its breaking up the home. Matt. 10:34-38. We are the light of the world. We must be different enough to *shine*. Matt. 5:14.

---

1. "There is no victory for us if we are resisting Christ."

2. "We must surrender not only the wrong things in our lives, but the right things, the best things in our lives."

— DR. CHARLES G. TRUMBULL

LESSON SEVENTEEN

The Victorious Life and Soul Winning

As Christ controls us, His passion for the salvation of the lost, which brought Him from the glory and took Him to the cross, will more and more manifest itself in our lives. Luke 19:10. As the love of God floods our lives, even as He "so loved the world" so will we, if not in omnipotent measure, at least in holy intensity. There can be no exception to this rule. Bring believers into victorious living, and the whole cause of evangelism and missions will be furthered. The whole world then becomes our parish in heart involvement and prayer interest. How eagerly will we want to serve in the place, great or small, to which He assigns us! How gladly will we give, to the limit of our ability, in strength and in money that one more "son" may be born into God's family, white, black, or yellow! For the victorious Christian *knows* that "except a man be born again he cannot see the kingdom of God" (John 3:3) — that nothing but a "new creature" really counts in the sight of God (Gal. 6:15).

1. The supreme task of the church is to evangelize the world, and, whether by public or personal evangelism, it finally does it by individuals winning individuals. That is the task for the individual Christians of each generation with its hundreds of millions of souls. What a task to stir the zeal and enthusiasm of those who love the Lord! A victorious Christian must be on fire in this cause. Mark 16:15; Rom. 10:13-15; I Cor. 9:22; Matt. 16:26; Acts 8:1, 4; Dan. 12:3; Ezek. 3:18, 19.

2. No one is truly evangelized until he has accepted Christ as his personal Saviour and Sin-bearer, on the ground of grace and apart from human works as a condition. It is our task and privilege to seek out the unsaved and *ask them to accept Christ,* and not to expect them to come by themselves. John 1:12, 13; Eph. 2:8-10; John 9:35.

3. As Timothy was evangelized (II Tim. 1:5; 3:15) and as the children in the churches of the Ephesians and Colossians were, so each child today should have that same opportunity. Paul, in addressing his letters to these churches, wrote to the children *as believers.* Eph. 1:1; 6:1, 2; Col. 1:2; 3:20.

4. It is the duty of parents to "nurture" their children "in the Lord." This means to evangelize them. Eph. 6:4. After His resurrection, Jesus *commanded* Peter to *feed* His (Jesus') *lambs.* These were the children of the church or Sunday school. The Peters of today should evangelize every child. John 21:15.

NOTES: 1. Jesus urged that we go out and seek the lost children as a true shepherd does his lost sheep and that we not despise them (their value and need). He declared that it is not the Father's will that *"one* of these little ones should perish." Matt. 18:10-14.

2. It takes no more faith to believe that a child will be "born again" when he accepts Christ than it does to believe that an adult will when he accepts the Lord. Christ asserts that little children do believe on Him. Many, many faithful Christians were truly regenerated at eight and ten years of age, and even younger. Matt. 18:6.

---

1. "It is very important to be perfectly clear on Jesus Christ as Saviour."

2. "Lord, you can have all there is of me."

— DR. CHARLES G. TRUMBULL

LESSON EIGHTEEN

The Victorious Life and Consecration for Service

While consecration for service may be included in our yielding for victory, it should be a very definite and distinct step. God is carrying on a mighty program in the world and He needs every believer in His service. Our Lord has a definite place of service for each individual as well as a special piece of work for him to accomplish. He is the "Head" of the "body," and it is His work to place each member. If we place ourselves, there may be too many "hands" and not enough "feet." Again, if He appoints us to fill the place of a "hand," He will see that we are fitted for that place and that we succeed there. What a tragedy for some "members" not to be "placed" or, having placed themselves, to be misfits. Many "members" are not "functioning" at all. I Cor. 12:17, 18. For these reasons there is a dearth of workers, especially in the undesirable and neglected places. Our consecration must be deep enough to enable and prompt us to serve anywhere, in the most difficult place if need calls. John 21:21, 22.

1. Full consecration is our "reasonable" service, in consideration of what He has done, what He is doing, and what He will do for us, and in view of the need of the unsaved millions. It requires the giving of ourselves with all that we possess to the Lord for all time to be used by Him as He may please. Rom. 12:1, 2; I Cor. 6:19, 20; II Cor. 5:14, 15.

2. Jesus taught full consecration as discipleship. The following were and are the requirements. If these conditions are not met we "cannot" be His disciples, though we may profess to be.

    a. A disciple must put God first — ahead of family, property, everything — even life itself. Luke 14:25, 26, 33.

b. A disciple must bear his "cross," make any needed sacrifice, go anywhere the Lord may send him. Luke 14:27.

c. A disciple must "count the cost," hold out faithful to the end and finish well — not hurt the cause by failing to endure. A disciple who quits is like salt that has "lost its savour." Luke 14:28-30, 34, 35.

d. A disciple must have faith to undertake the impossible, believing that God will make it possible even to fighting victoriously an army of 20,000 with an army of only 10,000. The Lord calls victorious Christians into just such service. Luke 14:31, 32.

3. The Lord gives special "gifts" (abilities) to *every* believer for service, thus showing that He expects each one to serve. Those who respond are amply equipped, for He bestows "grace" according to the *measure* of the gift. God bestows the gift, we must "stir" it up. Eph. 4:7, 8, 11; II Tim. 1:6.

NOTES: 1. Special power is given for service, and only in service will it be manifested. We must believe that it will come. If we are true disciples the power will always be given according to the need. The gift, the grace, and the power, each coming from God, make the performance of the service all of grace and exclude boasting over success. I Cor. 15:10; I Pet. 4:10, 11.

2. The Lord calls each disciple to his place of service and guides him in that service. Acts 13:2; 16:9.

------

1. "The Lord wants to run your life for you; He does not want you to run it for Him."

2. "We must surrender our loved ones, and I do not know of anything harder in the world to surrender than that. Some of us are letting our loved ones stand between us and Jesus Christ."

— DR. CHARLES G. TRUMBULL

LESSON NINETEEN

The Victorious Life and the Means of Grace

We are saved by grace and are kept saved by grace; we have victory by grace, and service is all of grace, yet there are many things which we must do. Such things as we may do have no saving power in them and no merit but they are vitally related to our continuing to appropriate the grace so freely offered. Then other believers, too weak to gather and apply the glorious truth, need our ministry. The unsaved also need to be brought to the source of grace. Every means of grace provided by God indicates that He knew we would need just that means of grace. "Let him that thinketh he standeth take heed lest he fall." I Cor. 10:12. If we think we are so strong that we can get along without the God-provided means of grace, we manifest a spiritual pride that questions God's wisdom and may prove our undoing. "Work out your own salvation, *with fear and trembling*" shows the danger of lapsing into a backslidden state. Phil. 2:12. All around us are examples of those who have "been overtaken in a fault." Gal. 6:1.

1. As truly as the Lord formed the Church, His body, so he established the local church, which in its most simple form is wherever two or three are gathered in Christ's name. We need the public assembly of believers — the Lord's presence is there; numbers encourage; the fellowship and the vocal expression of faith in song and testimony stimulate; the care and direction of leaders are needed. Matt. 18:20; Heb. 10:25; I Thess. 2:14; II Thess. 1:4; I Cor. 4:17.

2. We need the ministry of those whom God has "set in the church" for the "edifying of the body of Christ;" each one of them is for our help today, whether prophet (preacher), evangelist, teacher, pastor, exhorter, ruler, giver, one who shows mercy, or a helper. These

43

function mainly where believers gather together. Rom. 12:6-8; I Cor. 12:28; Eph. 4:11-13.

3. The prayerful reading of the Word of God is a wonderful means of grace. It should never be neglected. Not only should we read the Word, but we should meditate upon it. Ps. 1:2. We need to read the Word, for it reveals God to us; it feeds our faith; it shapes our conduct; it molds our doctrine; it abounds with promises we may claim. John 5:39; Deut. 11:18-20.

4. Intimate communion with God is a wonderful means of grace. It is blessed to have conscious fellowship with God. All prayer, and especially answered prayer, is a means of grace. John 14:21; Luke 18:1.

NOTES: 1. Communing with our own hearts in the Lord is a means of grace (Eph. 5:18-20), giving a testimony of God's salvation or goodness is another (Mal. 3:16), taking communion, where we show forth the Lord's death, is a third (I Cor. 11:25, 26).

2. The fellowship, counsel, and encouragement of fellow Christians and special Christian friends, are a great means of grace. Twice blessed are those whose life-companions are spiritual Christians. Phil. 1:8; Philemon 1, 7.

"Life becomes an utterly different thing for the Christian who is trusting Christ as Victor."

— DR. CHARLES G. TRUMBULL

LESSON TWENTY

The Victorious Life and the Value of Good Works

We are not saved by good works or kept victorious by good works; but victorious living will produce them in endless variety, and without fail. The best good works will always be those which have to do with rendering faithful service in the spiritual task to which the Lord has assigned us; in preaching or teaching, or soul-winning, or giving of our means to the advancement of the gospel. Certain good results always follow the gospel: honorable conduct; happy homes; better government; the emancipation of women; the care of the aged, the insane, and the lepers. While the winning of the lost is our primary task, Scripture very strongly commands and commends every form of good works which tends to relieve poverty and suffering.

1. We are saved by grace through faith, but each individual will receive rewards in glory according to his faithfulness and good works performed while here. Our bad works are held against us as well as our neglect of doing good works. II Cor. 5:10; I Cor. 3:8; Luke 6:23; Rev. 22:12; II Cor. 9:6-8.

2. Faithful temporal service will be rewarded. Eph. 6:5-8. Giving a drink of water in Jesus' name will be rewarded. Matt. 10:42. Some works count for more than others; some believers will receive no reward. They shall be saved "so as by fire." I Cor. 3:12-15.

3. The rewards offered are very, very great, even to sharing the reign with Christ. Rev. 3:21; 21:7; 22:3, 5; II Tim. 4:6-8; II Tim. 2:10, 12.

4. We are to be "zealous of good works" and "careful to maintain good works" (Titus 2:14; 3:8), and we are to "do good unto all men, especially unto them who are of the household of faith" (Gal. 6:10).

5. Intercessory prayer is a good work. Relieving the

widow and fatherless; extending hospitality even to strangers; restoring the wayward; supporting the weak; weeping with those who weep, and rejoicing with them who rejoice; helping the poor; caring for the sick; teaching the ignorant — all are numbered as good works. Rom. 15:30-32; James 1:27, Heb. 13:2; Gal. 6:1; I Thess. 5:14; Rom. 12:15.

NOTES: 1. Those who have little talent will receive as great reward as those who possess many talents, if they remain equally faithful. Those who put off becoming Christians lose reward which might have been theirs had they come to Christ earlier. When a child is won, both a soul and a life are saved. Matt. 25:15, 19-23.

2. It is only God's loving kindness that provides rewards. It is all of His grace. A great God would bestow only great rewards. The rewards which our God bestows are eternal. We are admonished to get our full reward. Luke 17:10; I Pet. 1:4; Dan. 12:3; II John 8.

"One thing we must remember is that the victorious life is a life of ease rather than effort, so far as the sin question is concerned. I do not mean to say that victorious-life Christians do not work hard — all those I know do — but they work *from* victory, not *for* victory."

— DR. CHARLES G. TRUMBULL

LESSON TWENTY-ONE

The Victorious Life — Its Scope

We are to be presented "faultless before the presence of his glory." Jude 24. We can and should be blameless here (I Thess. 5:23, 24), but it is our glorious destiny to be faultless in the glory. We are "created in Christ Jesus unto good works (perfect good works) which God hath before ordained that we should walk in them" (in eternity). Eph. 2:10. It is well for us to contemplate in a practical way that we are journeying toward a sinless heaven and that we are being prepared for it. God "is able to keep you from falling" because of "the exceeding greatness of his power *to us-ward who believe,* according to the working of his mighty power, which he wrought in Christ, when he raised him from the dead, and set him at his own right hand." Eph. 1:19, 20. There is no lack of power, and it is at our disposal, especially provided for our perfecting. Let us appropriate it in full measure.

1. In the future we are promised sinless spirits, we shall be in Christ's likeness, possessing glorified bodies, and we shall inherit an eternal heaven of perfect happiness. Heb. 12:22, 23; Rom. 8:11; I John 3:2; Rev. 21:1-4, 27; 22:5, 14.

2. Paul said, "I also labor, striving according to his working, which worketh in me mightily" — "warning every man, and teaching every man in all wisdom; that we may present *every man perfect* in Christ Jesus." The ministry gifts are for the "perfecting of the saints — till we all come .... unto a perfect man, *unto the measure of the stature of the fullness of Christ.*" This is God's plan. Col. 1:28, 29; Eph. 4:12, 13.

3. Our heavenly Father resorts to chastisement in order to make us "partakers of his holiness." Earlier in these studies we found that God does not always remove affliction, because it works "together for good," that we

may be "conformed to the image of his son" (Rom. 8:28, 29); sometimes, if need be, He even sends affliction. Chastisement is only child-training, which makes God's purpose in it clear. Heb. 12:5-11.

4. The victorious life is decidedly progressive "from faith to faith" and from "glory to glory." Rom. 1:17; II Cor. 3:18; Eph. 3:19; 4:15; I Thess. 3:12.

NOTES: 1. By abiding in Christ (that is, continuing in the victorious life), we bear "more fruit" and then "much fruit." It is the "much fruit" that glorifies God. The "Father purgeth" us, thereby causing us to bear "more fruit." In the purging, we again see chastisement. John 15:1-8.

2. Faith should "rest" in appropriation of God's promises of victory and not become disturbed either constantly or even occasionally. There is real "rest to the people of God." We should "labor" to enter it, committing the past, the present, and the future to Him, thus resting in His sufficient grace for all circumstances. Heb. 4:9-11; II Cor. 12:9.

"It is His victory that we triumph in. He makes it ours, but it is His first, last, and always; we never have to win the victory, He has won it for us."
— DR. CHARLES G. TRUMBULL

LESSON TWENTY-TWO

The Victorious Life and Its Dangers

The victorious life has dangers peculiar to itself, dangers which are very real. There must be a reason why so few are living the victorious life. Many new converts have had it but, because of insufficient instruction, have lost it and seem unable to regain it. Paul led his new converts, just out of heathendom, into the victorious life, thus proving that it is not necessary to wait for greater maturity in order to begin it. But Paul taught a victorious life constantly; his epistles abound with that teaching. In that way his converts maintained it. In a church where all, or nearly all, lived the victorious life and where it was taught, the new converts would continue in it. In our days there is a dearth of teaching on the victorious life, and still less concerning its dangers. One thing is sure, if we become anxious as to how we are to meet the next temptation, we will lose our victory. To get victory or to retain it, we must look to Jesus only.

1. One danger in the victorious life is when we fail. Some, when they sin, do not count their fall as sin because they do not want to admit failure. Others are so discouraged with failure that they think there is no use to claim victory again. When we sin it is evidence of our failure to trust Christ only or to keep completely surrendered to Him. The remedy in this case is to confess the sin as sin, accept forgiveness, and claim victory anew. Victory will come at once. I John 1:9; Rom. 12:9.

2. The place effort holds in the victorious life confuses many. Much of victory as in unlove and temper is obtained by looking to Christ alone. In physical temptations, etc., there must be a refusal, a turning away. Here the effort must be made, but Christ alone is the One in whom trust is placed, and thus the power of sin is found to be broken. In service it is the same. We must really

let Christ work *through us* as we pursue the task. Phil. 4:13; I Cor. 9:27; 15:58; 16:10, 13.

3. There is danger of being satisfied with present attainment, because the victory is so wonderful. Paul still pressed on, and he makes it plain that there is always more to attain. Phil. 3:10-15.

4. Spiritual pride is another danger, and when we have it, our victory is gone. Feeling superior to those who do not have victory, or who have made less spiritual advancement is a danger. As Paul advanced in victory he became the "least of all saints." We should remember that we are all, alike, "complete in *Him*." Phil. 2:1-3; Rom. 14:1-10; Eph. 3:8; Gal. 5:26.

NOTES: 1. To expect "feeling" and "thrills" always with victory is a mistake. To depend upon feeling is to look away from Christ. Only as we look to Christ alone are we able to appropriate His life.

2. There is danger of being dogmatic, in thinking that we have more spiritual knowledge than others. The victorious Christian possesses the most complete and full promise with regard to answered prayer, and there is a danger that he may lose his faith because *his* prayers are not answered *quickly,* or *immediately.* Some prayers are a long time being answered, regardless of who makes the request. John 15:7; Rom. 9:1-3; Eph. 6:18.

"Why, of course, one who has known the victorious life may have failures — not must have, but may have; and John tells us the remedy — (I John 1:9) — and then there is instantaneous restoration."

— DR. CHARLES G. TRUMBULL

LESSON TWENTY-THREE

The Victorious Life and the Conflict with Satan

Victory is to be obtained not only over the flesh and the world, but it must extend to overcoming the attacks of Satan. The devil attacks us personally, and he stirs others whom he can influence or control to oppress us. He not only attacks us as a "roaring lion," but transforms himself into "an angel of light" and his "ministers — as the ministers of righteousness." I Pet. 5:8, 9; II Cor. 11:14, 15. His "devices" have wrecked the faith of many (II Cor. 2:11) as he has trapped them in his "snare" (II Tim. 2:24-26) or by his "wiles" (Eph. 6:11). We are told to be "sober" (serious-minded, realizing the kind of adversary whom we have), to be "vigilant;" to "resist the devil and he will flee from you." James 4:7. "Whom resist steadfast" but "in the faith," that is to trust Christ alone for the wisdom to detect his schemes and for the strength to overcome. Just let Christ fight him. I Pet. 5:9; I John 4:4.

1. Jesus prayed that we should be kept from the "evil one." John 17:15, R.V. We are given explicit instructions as to the method of fighting him. It is a spiritual fight on a spiritual basis. The Lord has provided "armor" for us, but we must put it on and use it. In using this armor, we are to "be strong in the Lord" (not in ourselves) and "in the power of *his* might." Eph. 6:10, 11, 13-18.

2. Scripture represents Satan as possessing a world-wide, unseen government increasing in power as the age draws near to its close. One of the chief purposes of prophecy is to forewarn us of Satan's terrible deceits and successes in the last days. Eph. 2:2; 6:12; II Thess. 2:3, 7, 9, 10; Rev. 12:12.

3. Satan's success will result for a time in a terrible apostasy of the professing church. In the prophetical

Scriptures much teaching and warning is given to prepare us for those conditions. At that time God will bless and deal with the true remnant of faithful individuals. I Tim. 4:1-3; II Tim. 3:1-7; 4:3, 4; Rev. 3:20.

4. The progress of the apostasy outlined in Scripture is given in figurative language — leaven of the Pharisees and Sadducees (Mat. 16:11); doctrine of the Nicolaitanes (Rev. 2:6); way of Cain (Jude 11); error, doctrine, and way of Balaam (Rev. 2:14; II Pet. 2:15); Jezebel (Rev. 2:20); Antichrist (I John 4:1-3; II John 7; II Pet. 2:1, 2); man of sin and false prophet (II Thess. 2:3, 4; Rev. 13:4, 8).

NOTES: 1. No matter when or how Satan attacks us, no matter how great the apostasy, we can still be "kept by the power of God *through faith* unto salvation ready to be revealed in the last time." I Pet. 1:5.

2. Jesus said, "lo, I am with you *alway,* even unto the *end of the world* (or age)," so we can count on Christ's power for victory over Satan to the very end. Matt. 28:20.

"Let the Lord Jesus Christ resist the devil for you, and the devil will be defeated."

— DR. CHARLES G. TRUMBULL

LESSON TWENTY-FOUR

The Victorious Life and Our Future Outlook

How true of the victorious Christian, "as thy days, so shall thy strength be," for "the eternal God is thy refuge, and underneath are the everlasting arms." Deut. 33:25, 27. "No good thing will He withhold from them that walk uprightly." Ps. 84:11. For "the path of the just is as the shining light that shineth more and more unto the perfect day." Prov. 4:18. "In quietness and confidence shall be your strength" (Isa. 30:15), for "I will never leave thee nor forsake thee" (Heb. 13:5). "Thy youth is renewed like the eagle's." Ps. 103:5. "Though our outward man perish, yet the inward man is renewed day by day. For our light affliction, which is but for a moment, worketh for us a far more exceeding and eternal weight of glory." II Cor. 4:16, 17. For we are in the care, and under the power of "Him that is able to do exceeding abundantly above all that we ask or think." Eph. 3:20.

1. "To . . . . live is Christ" — with more service for Him, hence a greater reward; and "to die is gain." If we "depart" we shall "be with Christ," which is "very far better" (R.V.) than to remain here. The martyrs used to say that their persecutors only hastened their glorification. Phil. 1:21, 23.

2. Boundless fruit bearing is assured to those who "abide" in Christ, making them a joy to the Lord; and bringing to them the fullest joy attainable in this lifetime. John 15:5, 11.

3. An abundant entrance into the glory and a great reward awaits the victorious Christian. II Pet. 1:11; Rev. 3:21; 21:7; Matt. 13:43; James 1:12; I Pet. 1:4; 5:4; I Cor. 2:9.

4. The "blessed hope" of our Lord's return fills us with a glad thrill of anticipation. Jesus promised to re-

turn, and to return for us. Titus 2:13; I John 3:2, 3; John 14:3; Col. 3:4.

5. He did not tell us when He would return but He said that it would be soon, so that each generation of believers might have a share in the thrill of expectancy. Matt. 24:36; Rev. 22:20; I Thess. 1:10; Phil. 3:20; I Cor. 1:7.

NOTES: 1. We are to "love his appearing" for it is the "same Jesus" whom we love, and who is our "all and in all" who is coming back. II Tim. 4:6-8; Acts 1:11; I Pet. 1:8.

2. We know that His coming is "nearer;" we believe it is very near. How wonderful if it should be today, or even while we are here. Some may mock, but we believe. Truly, the outlook of the victorious Christian is marvelous. Heb. 10:25, 37; Matt. 24:42; II Pet. 3:3, 4; I Thess. 4:13-18.

---

1. "God wants people to have an easy life. Did you ever know that? — The only easy life is the saved, victorious life; every other life is hard."

2. "If His death saved us from the penalty of sin, His life, the living Christ now, can keep us safe, if we will let Him, from the power of sin."

— DR. CHARLES G. TRUMBULL

EXAMINATION QUESTIONS ON THE VICTORIOUS OR SPIRIT-FILLED LIFE

1. What is the victorious or spirit-filled life?

2. Discuss the indwelling of the Holy Spirit in the believer.

3. What three spheres does the victorious life cover?

4. Compare the victorious life with sinless perfection.

5. Give five Bible texts which promise victory.

6. Define "justification by faith."

7. How is justification by faith obtained?

8. Discuss "justification by faith" compared to "justification by works."

9. Give three Bible texts which teach justification by faith.

10. Name and discuss the two great mysteries involved in the victorious life.

11. When does a believer become a member of the body of Christ? When does Christ begin to indwell a believer?

12. Prove that victory is by faith not of works.

13. Show that victory is all of grace, not by faith and works but by faith alone.

14. Name and discuss some of the substitutes for real victory.

15. What two decisions are necessary in order to enter the victorious life?

16. Why is it that so many believers do not have the victorious life?

17. What is meant by not being under the law but under grace? How does this apply to the victorious life?

18. Why must the "self-life" be yielded if we are to have victory?

19. Show by the Scriptures that the victorious life is Christ living His life in us.

20. Why does the victorious life produce a life of love?

21. Why must our minds be renewed, and how does the victorious life bring this about?

22. What is meant in Scripture by "the old man" and what is done with him when we have victory?

23. Name the graces which adorn the victorious life. Do victorious Christians "grow" in these?

24. What should be the standard of conduct for the victorious Christian?

25. In sickness and affliction and persecution, name the two ways in which God may give victory.

26. Discuss the prayer life of a victorious Christian.

27. Since the victorious Christian must live a separated life, explain what the Bible teaches on separated living.

28. What place does soul winning take in the life of a victorious Christian and why?

29. Why should a victorious Christian be interested in child evangelism?

30. Define true consecration. Why is consecration so important?

31. What four things are required of a disciple of Christ?

32. Name and discuss two of the means of grace which the Lord has made available to saved people.

33. Name and discuss some of the good works which should manifest themselves in the life of a victorious Christian.

34. Is there a growth in the measure of victory, after victory is once a reality in the life? What is chastisement and from whom does it come and what is its purpose?

35. Discuss some of the dangers encountered in the victorious life.

36. Can the victorious life be lost? If so, how can it be regained?

37. Discuss the work of Satan, as it relates to the victorious Christian.

38. Discuss the future outlook of the victorious Christian.

39. Show that the victorious life is a life of "resting" rather than a life of "struggle."

40. What relation does the work of the Holy Spirit in a victorious Christian sustain to the work of the indwelling Christ?

TEACHER'S CERTIFICATES

The International Child Evangelism Fellowship is now offering a Teacher's Certificate to all who satisfactorily complete the prescribed course of study and spend one year in practice teaching in child evangelism classes, using one of the Fellowship courses of Bible studies for children.

A grade of 75 per cent is required on examinations conducted by the teacher of the local Teacher's Training Class on the following named books: Teacher's Introductory Bible Studies; Handbook on Child Evangelism; Open Air Child Evangelism; Children's Home Bible Class Movement; The Victorious or Spirit-Filled Life; The Teacher's Guide.

The Teacher of Teachers must send the grades of each applicant for a certificate, and a signed Fellowship Statement of Faith for both the Teacher of Teachers and the applicant.

56